ArtNotes

to accompany

Prebles'

ARTFORMS

EIGHTH EDITION

Patrick Frank

PEARSON
Prentice
Hall

Upper Saddle River, New Jersey 07458

© 2006 by PEARSON EDUCATION, INC.
Upper Saddle River, New Jersey 07458

ISBN 0-13-193089-3

Printed in the United States of America

Museum credits for fine art photos can be found with the images in the text.

Contents

Part One
Art Is . . .

DEER AND HANDS. Las Manos Cave, Argentina.
c. 1500 B.C.E. *(page 1)*

_____
_____
_____
_____
_____
_____
_____
_____
_____
_____
_____

Chapter One
The Nature of Art

Notes

1 Wassily Kandinsky. COMPOSITION IV. 1911.
(page 3)

2 WHEEL OF TIME. Tibetan sand mandala. 1997.
(page 4)

3 THE TREE OF JESSE. West façade, Chartres
Cathedral. c. 1150–1170. *(page 5)*

4 BLACKFEET PARFLECHE. 1885. *(page 6)*

5 DISH. 10th Century. East Iran. *(page 6)*

6 STONEHENGE. Wiltshire, England. c. 2000 B.C.E.
(page 7)

7 James Turrell. RODEN CRATER. Work in progress. 1988 to the present. *(page 8)*

8 DANCE WAND IN HONOR OF ESHU. Yoruba.
(page 8)

9 Rembrandt van Rijn. SELF-PORTRAIT. 1658.
(page 9)

10 Yong Soon Min. DWELLING. 1994. *(page 9)*

11 Romare Bearden. PREVALENCE OF RITUAL:
TIDINGS. 1967. *(page 10)*

12 Romare Bearden. ROCKET TO THE MOON. 1971. *(page 10)*

13 ROMARE BEARDEN. *(page 11)*

14 Francisco Goya. THE DISASTERS OF WAR, NO. 18: BURY THEM AND SAY NOTHING. 1818. *(page 12)*

15 Félix González-Torres. UNTITLED (DEATH BY GUN). 1990. *(page 12)*

16 Chaz Maviyane-Davies. OUR FEAR IS THEIR BEST WEAPON. 2002. *(page 13)*

17 DECORATIVE PANEL FROM THE ALHAMBRA. Granada. Nasrid Period, 14th Century. *(page 14)*

18 Miriam Schapiro. HEARTLAND. 1985. *(page 14)*

_____
_____
_____
_____
_____
_____
_____
_____
_____
_____
_____
_____

Chapter Two
Awareness, Creativity, and Communication

Notes

19 Edward Weston. PEPPER #30. 1930. *(page 17)*

_____
_____
_____
_____
_____
_____
_____
_____
_____
_____
_____

20 Leonardo da Vinci (1452–1519). A MAN TRICKED BY GYPSIES. c. 1493. *(page 18)*

_____
_____
_____
_____
_____
_____
_____
_____
_____
_____
_____

21 Otto Dix. DER KRIEG (WOUNDED SOLDIER). 1924. *(page 18)*

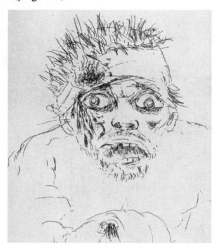

22 Vincent van Gogh. SKULL WITH A BURNING CIGARETTE. 1885–1886. *(page 19)*

23 Jean-Michel Basquiat. TOBACCO. 1984. *(page 19)*

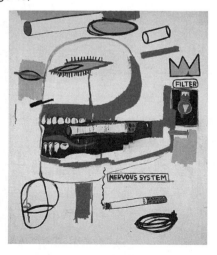

24 Kojyu, age 9. SEARCHING FOR BUGS IN THE PARK. *(page 20)*

25 FIRST LINES. *(page 20)*

26 Alana, age 2. HOUSE. *(page 20)*

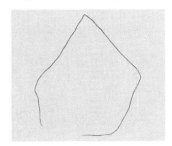

27 Alana, age 3. GRANDMA. *(page 20)*

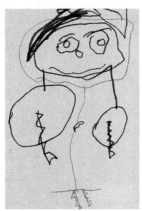

28 Jeff, age 3. HAND WITH LINE AND SPOTS. *(page 20)*

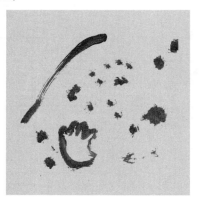

29 Jason, almost 4. MOTHER OCTOPUS WITH BABIES. *(page 21)*

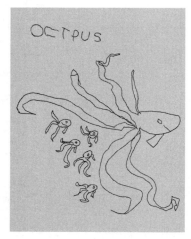

30 Yuki, age 8. I CAN RIDE, I CAN RIDE MY UNICYCLE. *(page 21)*

31 Anonymous Child. BIRDS. *(page 21)*

a. This picture shows one child's drawing of a bird before exposure to coloring books.

b. Then the child colored a workbook illustration.

c. After coloring the workbook birds, the child lost creative sensitivity and self-reliance.

32 Anna Zemankova. UNTITLED. ca, 1970s. *(page 23)*

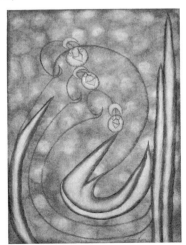

33 Sabatino "Simon" Rodia. **a.** NUESTRO
PUEBLO. Watts, California. 1921–1954. **b.** Detail
of NUESTRO PUEBLO. *(page 24)*

34 James Hampton. THRONE OF THE THIRD
HEAVEN OF THE NATION'S MILLENNIUM
GENERAL ASSEMBLY. c. 1950–1964. *(page 25)*

35 Arroyo Hondo Carver. OUR LADY OF THE
IMMACULATE CONCEPTION. 1830–1850. *(page 26)*

36 William Harnett. A SMOKE BACKSTAGE.
1877. *(page 27)*

37 René Magritte. LA TRAHISON DES IMAGES
(CECI N'EST PAS UNE PIPE). 1929. *(page 28)*

38 CHILKAT BLANKET. Tlingit, before 1928.
(page 28)

39 Theo van Doesburg (C.E.M. Kupper).
ABSTRACTION OF A COW. Studies for
composition (THE COW). c. 1916. *(page 29)*

Theo van Doesburg (C.E.M. Kupper). COMPOSITION
(THE COW) c. 1917 (*Dated* 1916). *(page 29)*

Theo van Doesburg (C.E.M. Kupper).
COMPOSITION (THE COW). c. 1917. *(page 29)*

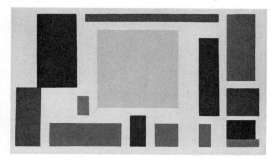

40 Nancy Graves. FOOTSCRAY, from the
AUSTRALIAN SERIES. 1985. *(page 30)*

41 TUKUTUKU PANELS. Maori peoples, New
Zealand. 1930s. *(page 30)*

 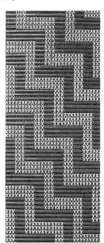

42 François Auguste René Rodin. THE KISS.
1886. *(page 31)*

43 Constantin Brancusi. THE KISS. c. 1916.
(page 31)

44 VISUAL METAPHOR. Student Project. *(page 32)*

45 Elliott Erwitt. FLORIDA. 1968. *(page 32)*

46 Georgia O'Keeffe. ORIENTAL POPPIES. 1927.
(page 33)

47 Georgia O'Keeffe. JACK-IN-THE-PULPIT NO. V.
1930. *(page 33)*

48 Yousuf Karsh. GEORGIA O'KEEFFE. 1956.
(page 34)

49 Albrecht Dürer. THE KNIGHT, DEATH AND THE DEVIL. 1513. *(page 35)*

50 DESCENT OF THE GANGES. Māmallapuram, India. 7th Century. **a.** Overview. *(page 36)*
b. Detail. *(page 37)*

51 Betye Saar. THE LIBERATION OF AUNT JEMIMA. 1972. *(page 38)*

52 Carlos Frésquez. MI CASA ES SU CASA:
YELLOW WALL (WEST). 1997. *(page 38)*

Part Two
The Language of Visual Experience

Notes

Claes Oldenburg and Coosje van Bruggen.
SHUTTLECOCKS. 1994. *(page 39)*

Chapter Three
Visual Elements

53 Paul Klee. LANDSCAPE WITH YELLOW BIRDS. 1923. *(page 40)*

54 Ansel Adams. RAILS AND JET TRAILS, ROSEVILLE, CALIFORNIA. 1953. *(page 41)*

55 LINE VARIATIONS. *(page 41)*

a. Actual line.

b. Implied line.

c. Actual straight lines and implied curved line.

d. Line created by an edge.

e. Vertical line (attitude of alert attention); horizontal line (attitude of rest).

f. Diagonal lines (slow action, fast action).

g. Sharp, jagged line.

h. Dance of curving lines.

i. Hard line, soft line.

j. Ragged, irregular line.

56 Abby Leigh. WALLENOTE, 2002. *(page 42)*

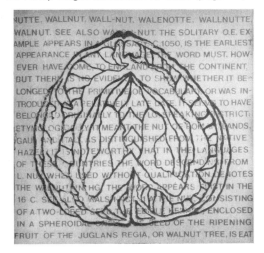

57 Bridget Riley. CURRENT. 1964. *(page 42)*

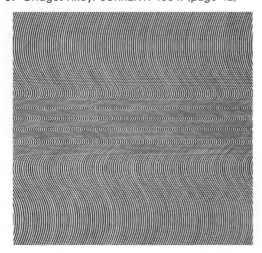

58 Jackson Pollock. DRAWING. 1950. *(page 42)*

59 Alexander Calder. TWO ACROBATS. 1928.
(page 42)

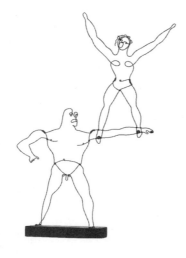

60 Duane Preble. BLUE GINGER. 1993. *(page 43)*

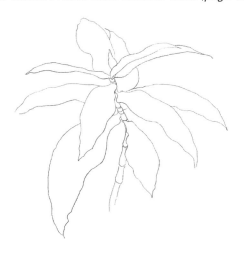

61 Attributed to Torii Kiyonobu I. WOMAN
DANCER WITH FAN AND WAND. c. 1708. *(page 43)*

62 Torii Kiyotada. AN ACTOR OF THE ICHIKAWA
CLAN IN A DANCE MOVEMENT OF VIOLENT
MOTION. c. 1715. *(page 43)*

63 John Sloan. THE FLUTE PLAYER. 1905.
(page 43)

64 Marc Chagall. I AND THE VILLAGE. 1911.
(page 44)

64b

65 A SHAPE OF SPACE. (implied shape).
(page 45)

66 Duane Preble. NIGHT LIFE (figure-ground reversal). *(page 45)*

67 M. C. Escher. SKY AND WATER I. 1938. *(page 45)*

68 QENNEFER, STEWARD OF THE PALACE. c. 1450 B.C.E. *(page 46)*

69 Alberto Giacometti. MAN POINTING. 1947. *(page 46)*

70 Elizabeth Catlett. BREAD, 1962. *(page 47)*

71a. Cesar Pelli and Associates. NORTH TERMINAL RONALD REAGAN WASHINGTON NATIONAL AIRPORT. 1997. **b.** CLOSE-UP INTERIOR. *(page 48)*

72 POND IN A GARDEN. Wall painting from the
tomb of Nebamun. Egypt. c. 1400 B.C.E. *(page 49)*

73 CLUES TO SPATIAL DEPTH. *(page 50)*

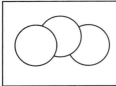

a. Overlap.

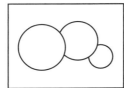

b. Overlap and
diminishing size.

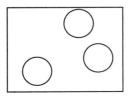

c. Vertical placement.

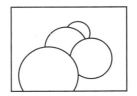

d. Overlap, vertical placement,
and diminishing size.

74 Mu Qi. SIX PERSIMMONS. c. 1269. *(page 50)*

75 LINEAR PERSPECTIVE. *(page 51)*

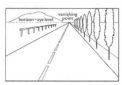

a. One-point linear perspective.

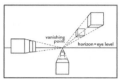

b. One-point linear perspective. Cubes above eye level, at eye level, and below eye level.

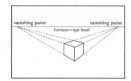

c. Two-point linear perspective.

76 Raphael. THE SCHOOL OF ATHENS. 1508.
76b Raphael. THE SCHOOL OF ATHENS. 1508. *(page 52)*

Perspective lines showing eye level, main vanishing point, and left vanishing point for the stone block in the foreground.

77 Study of Raphael's *The School of Athens*. *(page 52)*

78 Asher Brown Durand. KINDRED SPIRITS.
1849. *(page 53)*

79 Shen Zhou. POET ON A MOUNTAIN TOP (CHANGI–LI
YUAN–T'IAO). Series: LANDSCAPE ALBUM: FIVE LEAVES
by Shen Zhou, ONE LEAF by Wen Cheng–Ming (Shen
Shih–t'ien Wen Cheng-ming shan-shui-ho-chuan).
Ming Dynasty (1368–1644). *(page 54)*

80 ISOMETRIC PERSPECTIVE. *(page 54)*

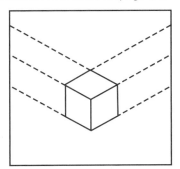

81 Anonymous. EIGHTEEN SCHOLARS. Detail.
Song Dynasty (960–1279). *(page 54)*

82 AZTEC CALENDAR STONE. 1479. *(page 55)*

83 Sassetta and Workshop of Sassetta. THE
MEETING OF SAINT ANTHONY AND SAINT PAUL.
c. 1440. *(page 55)*

84 Kristin Jones and Andrew Ginzel.
MNEMONICS. 1992. *(page 56)*

85 Harold Edgerton. MILK SPLASH RESULTING
FROM DROPPING A BALL. 1936. *(page 56)*

86 DANCING KRISHNA. Tanjor, Tamil Nadu.
South India. Chola Dynasty. c. 1300. *(page 57)*

87 Thomas Eakins. MAN POLE VAULTING. 1884.
(page 57)

88 Jenny Holzer. UNTITLED (Selections from
Truisms, Inflammatory Essays, The Living
Series, The Survival Series, Under a Rock,
Laments, and Child Text), 1989. *(page 58)*

89 Alexander Calder. BIG RED. 1959. *(page 58)*

90 Daniel Chester French. ABRAHAM LINCOLN, detail of seated figure, 1922. *(page 59)*

a. As originally lit by daylight.

b. With the addition of artificial light.

91 DARK/LIGHT RELATIONSHIPS. Value scale compared to uniform middle gray. *(page 59)*

92 DRAWING OF LIGHT ON A SPHERE. *(page 60)*

93 Annibale Carracci. HEAD OF A YOUTH. *(page 60)*

94 Dan Flavin. UNTITLED, 1996. *(page 61)*

95 WHITE LIGHT REFRACTED BY A PRISM. *(page 62)*

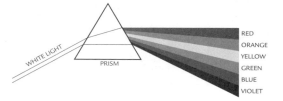

96 THE THREE DIMENSIONS OF COLOR. *(page 63)*

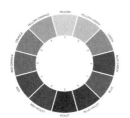

a. *Hue*—the color wheel.

b. *Value*—from light to dark.

Value scale from white to black.

Value variation in red.

c. *Intensity*—from bright to dull.

97 PIGMENT PRIMARIES: SUBTRACTIVE COLOR MIXTURE. *(page 64)*

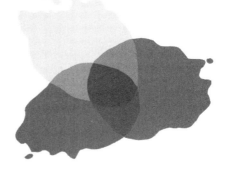

98 LIGHT PRIMARIES: ADDITIVE COLOR MIXTURE. *(page 64)*

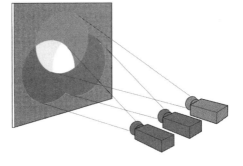

99 WARM/COOL COLORS. *(page 64)*

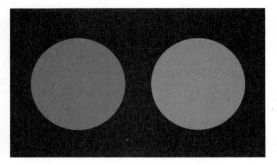

100 OPTICAL COLOR MIXTURE. Detail of Georges Seurat's A SUNDAY ON LA GRANDE JATTE, 1884–86. *(page 65)*

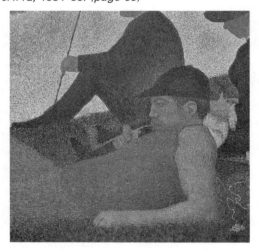

101a–h Color printing detail of Sandro Botticelli's BIRTH OF VENUS, 1486. *(page 66)*

102 James Abbott McNeill Whistler. NOCTURNE:
BLUE AND GOLD—OLD BATTERSEA BRIDGE.
1872–1875. *(page 67)*

103 Jennifer Bartlett. VOLVO COMMISSION.
1984. *(page 67)*

104 Keith Haring. UNTITLED. 1982. *(page 68)*

105 Meret Oppenheim. OBJECT (LE DEJEUNER EN FOURRURE). 1936. *(page 69)*

106 FLASK. China, Tang Dynasty, 9th century. *(page 69)*

107 Vincent van Gogh. Detail of STARRY NIGHT. 1889. *(page 70)*

108 Jan van Eyck. Detail of THE MARRIAGE OF
GIOVANNI ARNOLFINI AND GIOVANNA CENAMI.
1434. *(page 71)*

Chapter Four
Principles of Design

109 Jacob Lawrence. GOING HOME. 1946. *(page 74)*

110 Pieter de Hooch. INTERIOR OF A DUTCH HOUSE. 1658. *(page 74)*

111 Alberto Giacometti. CHARIOT. 1950. *(page 75)*

112 James Hoban. A DESIGN FOR THE PRESIDENT'S HOUSE. 1792. **a.** Elevation. *(page 75)* **b.** WHITE HOUSE. Front view. 1997. *(page 75)*

113 PORTRAIT OF THE HUNG-CHIH EMPEROR. Ming Dynasty, 15th Century. *(page 76)*

114 Suzuki Haranobu. THE EVENING GLOW OF THE ANDO, from the series EIGHT PARLOR VIEWS. Edo period. 1766. *(page 77)*

115 Nicolas Poussin. THE HOLY FAMILY ON THE STEPS. 1648. *(page 78)*

116 Edgar Degas. JOCKEYS BEFORE THE RACE. c. 1878–1879. *(page 79)*

117 Beverly Pepper. EXCALIBUR. 1975–1976. *(page 80)*

118 Francisco Goya. BULLFIGHT: THE AGILITY AND DARING OF JUANITO APINANI. *(page 81)*

a.   **b.**   **c.**

119 LUSTER-PAINTED BOWL. Hispano-Moresque, Manises. Spain. c. 1400. *(page 82)*

120 Raphael Sanzio. MADONNA OF THE CHAIR.
c. 1514. *(page 83)*

121 Ogata Korin. CRANES, c. 1700. *(page 83)*

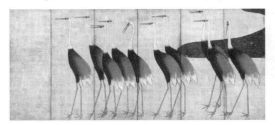

122 José Clemente Orozco. ZAPATISTAS. 1931.
(page 84)

123 Claes Oldenburg and Coosje van Bruggen.
SHUTTLECOCKS. 1994. *(page 85)*

124 SCALE RELATIONSHIPS. *(page 85)*

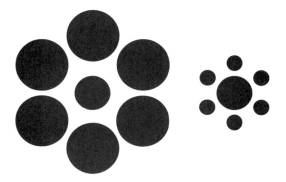

125 Rembrandt van Rijn. SELF-PORTRAIT IN A CAP,
OPEN MOUTHED AND STARING. 1630. *(page 85)*

126 Michelangelo Buonarroti. PIETÀ. 1501. *(page 86)*

127 Master of the Beautiful Madonna. PIETÀ.
c. 1415. *(page 87)*

128 Henri Matisse. Photographs of three
states of LARGE RECLINING NUDE.   **a.** State I,
May 3, 1935.   **b.** State IX, May 29, 1935.
c. State XII, September 4, 1935. *(page 88)*

129 Henri Matisse. LARGE RECLINING NUDE.
1935. *(page 89)*

130 Henri Matisse. SELF-PORTRAIT, THREE-QUARTER
VIEW. 1948. *(page 90)*

Chapter 5
Evaluating Art

Notes

131 Elizabeth Vigee-Lebrun. SELF-PORTRAIT IN A STRAW HAT, 1782. *(page 92)*

_____

_____

_____

_____

_____

_____

_____

_____

_____

_____

_____

_____

132 Dawn Marie Jigagian. SHY GLANCE. 1976. *(page 92)*

_____

_____

_____

_____

_____

_____

_____

_____

_____

_____

_____

133 Titian. PIETÁ, 1576. *(page 94)*

134 Attributed to Dasavanta and Tara. UMAR
SLAYS A DRAGON, 1567–72. *(page 95)*

135 Ni Zan. SIX GENTLEMEN (SIX TREES), 1345.
(page 95)

136 PETER PLAGENS *(page 97)*

137 Frank Modell. © The New Yorker Collection, 1983. *(page 98)*

Part Three
The Media of Art

Notes

Carrie Mae Weems. ANCIENT RUINS OF TIME, FROM SERIES DREAMING IN CUBA, 2002. *(page 99)*

_____

_____

_____

_____

_____

_____

_____

_____

_____

_____

_____

Chapter Six
Drawing

138 Pamela Davis Kivelson. CAROL. 1973. *(page 100)*

139 Leonardo da Vinci. THREE SEATED FIGURES AND STUDIES OF MACHINERY. c. 1490. *(page 101)*

140 Iris Chamberlain, age 8. DESIGNS FOR
INVENTIONS. 1992. *(page 101)*

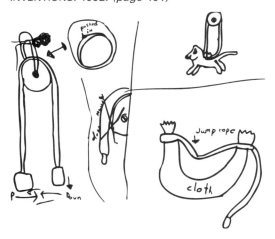

141 Elizabeth Layton. THE EYES OF THE LAW.
1985. *(page 102)*

142 Vincent van Gogh. CARPENTER. c. 1880.
(page 103)

143 Vincent van Gogh. OLD MAN WITH HIS HEAD IN HIS HANDS. 1882. *(page 103)*

144 Vincent van Gogh. SELF PORTRAIT WITH GRAY HAT. 1887. *(page 104)*

145 Michelangelo Buonarotti. Studies for the LIBYAN SIBYL on the Sistine Chapel ceiling. c. 1510. *(page 105)*

146 Pablo Picasso. FIRST COMPOSITION STUDY
FOR GUERNICA. May 1, 1937. *(page 106)*

147 Pablo Picasso. COMPOSITION STUDY FOR
GUERNICA. May 9, 1937. *(page 106)*

148 Pablo Picasso. GUERNICA. 1937. *(page 106)*

149 TYPES OF HATCHING. *(page 107)*

a. Hatching.

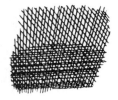

b. Cross-hatching.

c. Contour hatching.

150 Charles White. PREACHER. 1952. *(page 107)*

151 DRAWING TOOLS AND THEIR CHARACTERISTIC LINES. *(page 108)*

152 Judith Murray. OBSIDIAN. 1988. *(page 108)*

153 Georgia O'Keeffe. BANANA FLOWER. 1933.
(page 109)

154 Georges Pierre Seurat. L'ECHO, STUDY FOR
UNE BAIGNADE, ASNIERES. 1882–1891. *(page 109)*

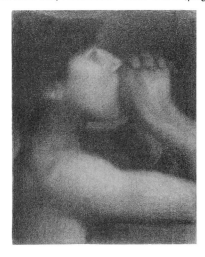

155 Rosalba Carriera. ALLEGORY OF PAINTING. c. 1720. *(page 110)*

156 Edgar Degas. LE PETIT DEJEUNER APRES LE BAIN (JEUNE FEMMME S'ESSUYANT). c. 1894. *(page 110)*

157 Vincent van Gogh. THE FOUNTAIN IN THE HOSPITAL GARDEN. 1889. *(page 111)*

158 Hokusai. TUNING THE SAMISEN. c. 1820–1825.
(page 112)

159 Rembrandt van Rijn. SASKIA ASLEEP. c. 1642.
(page 112)

160 Julie Mehretu. BACK TO GONDWANALAND.
(page 113)

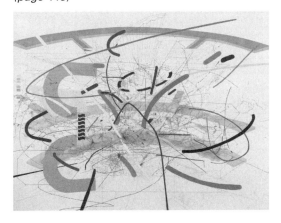

161 Christine Hiebert, UNTITLED, 2004. *(page 114)*

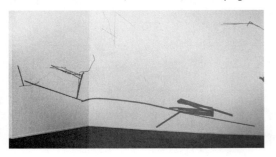

162 John Currin. HOBO. 1999. *(page 114)*

163 John Currin. HOBO. 2001. *(page 114)*

Chapter Seven
Painting

Notes

164 Gerhard Richter. ABSTRACT PAINTING
(551–4). 1984. *(page 116)*

165 Winslow Homer. SLOOP, NASSAU. 1899.
(page 117)

166 Qi Baishi. LANDSCAPE. 1924. *(page 118)*

167 Fra Filippo Lippi. MADONNA AND CHILD.
c. 1440–1445. *(page 119)*

168 Jan van Eyck. MADONNA AND CHILD WITH
THE CHANCELLOR ROLIN. c. 1433–1434. *(page 120)*

169 Rembrandt van Rijn. Detail of SELF-
PORTRAIT. 1663. *(page 121)*

170 Frank Auerbach. HEAD OF MICHAEL PODRO.
1981. *(page 121)*

171 Joan Mitchell. BORDER. 1989. *(page 122)*

172 Inka Essenhigh. ESCAPE POD, 2003.
(page 122)

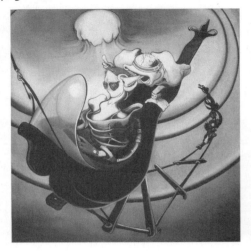

173 David Hockney. A BIGGER SPLASH. 1967.
(page 123)

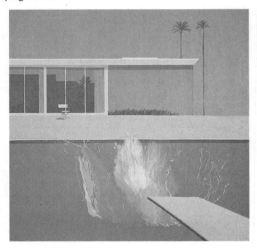

174 Audrey Flack. WHEEL OF FORTUNE. 1977–1978.
(page 123)

175 PORTRAIT OF A BOY. From Fayum, Lower
Egypt. c. 50–100 C.E. *(page 124)*

176 Diego Rivera. Detail from DETROIT
INDUSTRY. 1932–1933. *(page 125)*

177 Diego Rivera. DETROIT INDUSTRY,
1932–1933. *(page 125)*

178 Judy Baca, director; Isabel Castro, designer. GREAT WALL OF LOS ANGELES, IMMIGRANT CALIFORNIA. 1976–1983. *(page 126)*

_____

_____

_____

_____

_____

_____

_____

_____

_____

_____

_____

Chapter Eight
Printmaking

Notes

179 Section of THE DIAMOND SUTRA. Chinese Buddhist text, 868. *(page 128)*

180 Katsushika Hokusai. THE WAVE. c. 1830. *(page 129)*

181 Emil Nolde. PROPHET. 1912. *(page 129)*

182 Elizabeth Catlett. SHARECROPPER. 1970. *(page 130)*

183 RELIEF. *(page 130)*

184 INTAGLIO. *(page 130)*

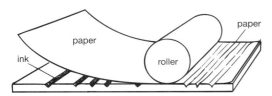

185 Albrecht Dürer. THE KNIGHT, DEATH AND THE DEVIL. 1513. *(page 130)*

186 Vija Celmins. UNTITLED (WEB 3), 2002. *(page 132)*

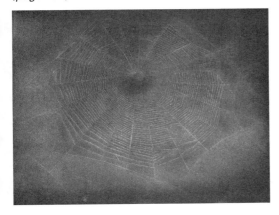

187 DRYPOINT PLATE. *(page 132)*

ink

188 Rembrandt Harmensz van Rijn. CHRIST PREACHING. c. 1652. *(page 133)*

189 Kitagawa Utamaro. A COMPETITIVE SHOWING OF BEAUTIES: HINZAURU OF THE HEIZETSURO. c. 1796. *(page 134)*

190 Mary Cassatt. THE LETTER. 1891. *(page 134)*

191 Honoré Daumier. RUE TRANSNONAIN, April 15, 1834. *(page 135)*

192 LITHOGRAPHY. *(page 136)*

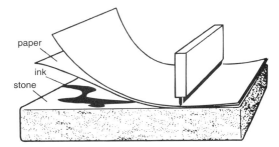

paper
ink
stone

193 Henri de Toulouse-Lautrec. JANE AVRIL.
c. 1893. *(page 136)*

194 Henri de Toulouse-Lautrec. JANE AVRIL
DANSANT. c. 1893. *(page 136)*

195 Henri de Toulouse-Lautrec. JANE AVRIL.
JARDIN DE PARIS. c. 1893. *(page 137)*

Notes

196 SCREENPRINTING. (page 138)

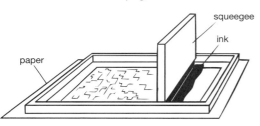

197 Andy Warhol. LITTLE RACE RIOT. 1964. *(page 138)*

198 Elizabeth Murray. EXILE, 1993. *(page 138)*

199 Willie Cole. STOWAGE. 1997. *(page 139)*

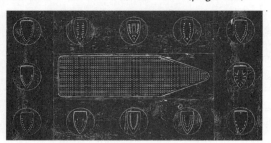

200 Alicia Candiani. LA HUMANIDAD, 2004. *(page 139)*

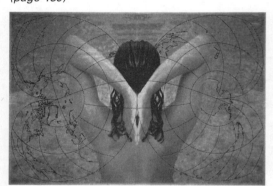

Chapter Nine
Camera Arts and Digital Imaging

Notes

201 EVOLUTION OF THE CAMERA OBSCURA, PREDECESSOR OF THE MODERN CAMERA. **a.** Sixteenth-century camera obscura. **b.** Seventeenth-century portable camera obscura. **c.** Seventeenth–nineteenth-century table model camera obscura. *(page 142)*

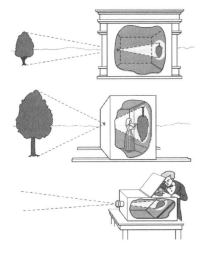

202 Louis Jacques Mandé Daguerre. LE BOULEVARD DU TEMPLE. 1839. *(page 143)*

203 Julia Margaret Cameron. JULIA JACKSON.
1866. *(page 144)*

204 Alfred Stieglitz. THE FLATIRON BUILDING.
1903. *(page 145)*

205 Henri Cartier-Bresson. BEHIND THE GARE
ST. LAZARE, PARIS. 1932. *(page 145)*

206 Man Ray. RAYOGRAPH, 1927. *(page 146)*

207 Lewis Hine. COAL BREAKERS, PENNSYLVANIA. 1910. *(page 146)*

208 MARGARET BOURKE-WHITE ATOP THE CHRYSLER BUILDING. 1934. *(page 147)*

209 Ansel Adams. CLEARING WINTER STORM, YOSEMITE NATIONAL PARK, CALIFORNIA. 1944. *(page 148)*

210 Eliot Porter. BLUE CLIFF, AZTEC CREEK, LAKE POWELL, UTAH, May 13, 1965. *(page 149)*

211 Wallace Berman. UNTITLED (B-3 MASTERLOCK), 1965. *(page 149)*

212 Sonia Landy Sheridan. FLOWERS. 1976.
(page 150)

213 Eadweard Muybridge. GALLOPING HORSE.
1878. *(page 151)*

214 Thomas Edison and W. K. Dickson. FRED
OTT'S SNEEZE. 1889. *(page 151)*

215 D. W. Griffith. INTOLERANCE. 1916.
a. Close-up ("Little Dear One").   **b.** Longshot
(Belshazzar's Feast). *(page 152)*

216 Sergei Eisenstein. THE BATTLESHIP
POTEMKIN. 1925. *(page 153)*

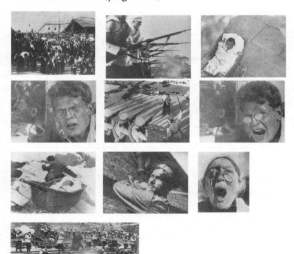

217 Charlie Chaplin. CITY LIGHTS. 1931. *(page 154)*

218 Orson Welles. CITIZEN KANE. 1941. *(page 154)*

219 Federico Fellini. LA DOLCE VITA. 1961. *(page 155)*

220 Walt Disney. FANTASIA. 1940. *(page 156)*

221 George Lucas. Still from STAR WARS, 1977. *(page 156)*

222 Still from PRINCESS MONONOKE. 1997. *(page 157)*

223 Still from JU DOU. 1990. *(page 157)*

224 Still from I, ROBOT. 2004. *(page 157)*

225 Nam June Paik and John Godfrey.
GLOBAL GROOVE. Video. *(page 158)*

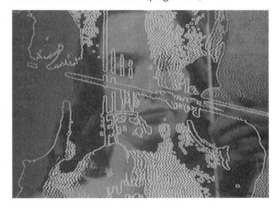

226 Joan Jonas. VOLCANO SAGA. 1987. *(page 159)*

227 Dara Birnbaum. HOSTAGE. 1994. *(page 159)*

228 Vera Molnar. *Parcours:* (MAQUETTE FOR AN ARCHITECTURAL ENVIRONMENT). 1976. *(page 160)*

229 Joseph Nechvatal. THE INFORMED MAN. 1986. *(page 160)*

230 Camilla Benolirao Griggers. ALIENATIONS
OF THE MOTHER TONGUE. 1996. *(page 161)*

231 William Latham. CR3Z72. 1992. *(page 161)*

232 Constance de Jong, Tony Oursler,
Stephen Vitiello. Screenshot from FANTASTIC
PRAYERS, 2000. *(page 162)*

233 Annette Weintraub, Screenshot from THE MIRROR THAT CHANGES. 2003. *(page 163)*

234 James Johnson. ONE THOUSAND WORDS. 1998. *(page 163)*

CRITERION	HERESY
MOODY	LICENSE
REGRET	INTRUDE
PERSERVERE	DANGER

Chapter Ten
Graphic Design and Illustration

Notes

235 Aleksandr Rodchenko and Vladimir Maiakovskii. GIVE ME SUN AT NIGHT. Design for Poster, 1923. *(page 165)*

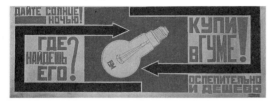

236 Cassandre (Adolpe Jean-Marie Noreau). L'ATLANTIQUE. 1932. *(page 166)*

237 Eric Rodenbeck. THE EMPTY CITY. 2000.
(page 166)

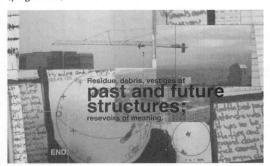

238 Landor Associates. ALTRIA LOGO, 2003.
(page 167)

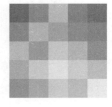

239 NASA LETTERHEAD STATIONERY. *(page 167)*

b. 1974. Designers Danne
& Blackburn, NYC. 1973

a. 1959. Logo
designer James
Modarelli.

c. 1992. Logo designer
James Modarelli.

240 Herb Lubalin, assisted by Alan Peckolick
and Tom Carnase. MOTHER & CHILD, logo for a
magazine (never produced). 1965. *(page 168)*

241 Tobias Frere-Jones. THREE TYPEFACES: NOBEL™,
ARMADA™, GARAGE GOTHIC™.1992–1994. *(page 168)*

Nobel

Armada

Garage Gothic

242 Heidi Cody. AMERICAN ALPHABET, 2000.
(page 169)

243 SILENCE=DEATH. 1986. *(page 169)*

244 Chaz Maviyane-Davies. RIGHTS, ARTICLE 15. 1996. *(page 169)*

245 Chaz Maviyane-Davies. ABSOLUTE POWER. Offset poster. 2002. *(page 170)*

246 Chaz Maviyane-Davies. *(page 170)*

247 Maira Kalman. NEWYORKISTAN. *(page 171)*

248 Jonathan Barnbrook. TOMAHAWK FONT
SAMPLE. 2003. *(page 171)*

249 NORTH AMERICAN TOUR '94. Poster. 1994.
(page 171)

250 Jamie Reid. GOD SAVE THE QUEEN. 1977.
(page 172)

251 David Carson. PAGES FROM RAY GUN
MAGAZINE. 1993. *(page 172)*

252 José Guadalupe Posada. LAS BRAVÍSIMAS
CALAVERAS GUATEMALTECAS DE MORA DE
MORALES. 1907. *(page 173)*

253 Norman Rockwell. MUSEUM WORKER. Cover for
SATURDAY EVENING POST, March 2, 1946. *(page 173)*

254 Maurice Sendak. READING IS FUN. *(page 174)*

Chapter Eleven
Sculpture

255 Alexander Calder. OBUS. 1972. *(page 175)*

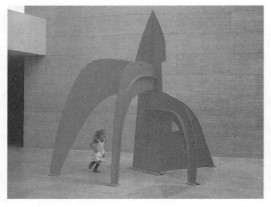

256 APOLLO. c. 415 B.C.E. *(page 175)*

257 ARMY ON THE MARCH. Angkor Wat, c. 1150, Cambodia. 1100–1150. *(page 176)*

258 Robert Longo. Middle portion, CORPORATE WARS: WALL OF INFLUENCE. 1982. *(page 176)*

259 DOUBLE FIGURE, MALE AND FEMALE. Maya. c. 700 C.E. *(page 177)*

260 Robert Arneson. CALIFORNIA ARTIST. 1982.
(page 177)

261 Scott Chamberlin. AHYRE. 1998. *(page 178)*

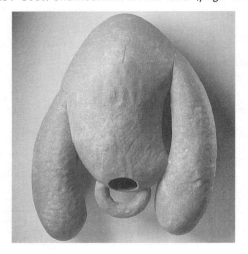

262 Duane Hanson. MUSEUM GUARD. 1975.
(page 179)

263 Charles Ray. SELF-PORTRAIT. 1990. *(page 179)*

264 Rachel Whiteread. PUBLIC ART FUND WATERTOWER PROJECT. 1997. *(page 180)*

265 Michelangelo Buonarroti. AWAKENING SLAVE. 1530–1534. *(page 181)*

266 MASSIVE STONE HEAD. 12th–10th centuries B.C.E. Olmec. *(page 181)*

267 Elizabeth Catlett. MOTHER AND CHILD #2. 1971. *(page 182)*

268 BODHISATTVA GUAN YIN. 11th–12th century. Northern Song (960–1127) or Liao Dynasty (916–1125). *(page 183)*

269 Julio González. MATERNITY. 1934. *(page 183)*

270 Julio González. THE MONTSERRAT. 1936–1937. *(page 183)*

271 Deborah Butterfield. NAHELE. 1986. *(page 184)*

272 Pablo Picasso. BULL'S HEAD. 1943. *(page 185)*

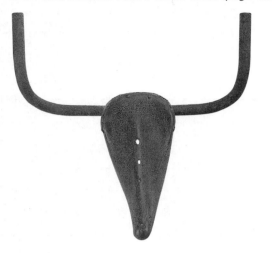

273 Roberto Visani. TRIBAL WAR. YOU SEE THE HUT YET YOU ASK "WHERE SHALL I GO FOR SHELTER." 2000–2003. *(page 185)*

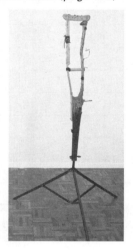

274 Alexander Calder. UNTITLED. 1976. *(page 186)*

275 Cai Guo Qiang. BORROWING YOUR
ENEMY'S ARROWS. 1998. *(page 187)*

276 Ouattara. HIP-HOP, JAZZ, MAKOUSSA, 1994.
(page 187)

277 Marisol. WOMEN AND DOG. 1964. *(page 188)*

278 Nam June Paik. INTERNET DWELLER: WOL.FIVE.YDPB. 1994. *(page 189)*

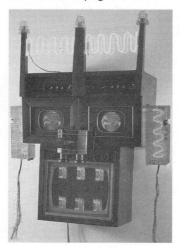

279 Ilya Kabakov. THE MAN WHO FLEW INTO SPACE FROM HIS APARTMENT. 1981–1988. *(page 189)*

280 James Turrell MEETING. 1980–1986. *(page 190)*

Chapter Twelve
Clay, Glass, Metal, Wood, Fiber

Notes

281 Miriam Schapiro. PERSONAL APPEARANCE #3. 1973. *(page 192)*

282 TEA BOWL. Satsuma ware. 17th century. *(page 193)*

283 Kakiemon V. BELL-FLOWER-SHAPED BOWL.
17th century. *(page 193)*

284 NAMPEYO DECORATING POTTERY. 1901.
(page 194)

285 Peter Voulkos. GALLAS ROCK. 1960. *(page 195)*

286 Toshiko Takaezu. MAKAHA BLUE II, 2002.
(page 196)

287 Dale Chihuly. MAUVE SEAFORM SET WITH BLACK
LIP WRAPS FROM THE "SEAFORMS" SERIES. 1985.
(page 197)

288 D'ARENBERG BASIN. Syria. Mid-13th century.
(page 197)

289 Albert Raymond Paley. PORTAL GATES. 1974. *(page 198)*

290 Virginia Dotson. CROSS WINDS. 1989. *(page 199)*

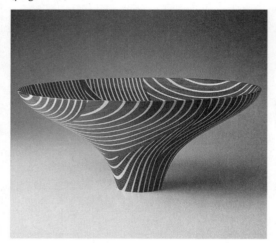

291 Sam Maloof. DOUBLE ROCKING CHAIR. 1992. *(page 199)*

292 THE ARDABIL CARPET. Tabriz. 1540. *(page 200)*

293 Diane Itter. PATTERN SCAPE. 1985. *(page 200)*

294 Jessie Pettway. BARS AND STRING-PIECE COLUMNS. 1950s. *(page 201)*

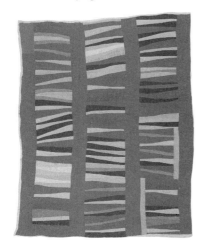

295 Polly Apfelbaum. BLOSSOM. 2000. *(page 201)*

296 Olga de Amaral. GOLD MOUNTAIN. 1992. *(page 202)*

297 Faith Ringgold. MRS. JONES AND FAMILY. 1973. *(page 202)*

298 Magdalena Abakanowicz. BACKS (IN
LANDSCAPE). 1976–1982. *(page 203)*

299 Faith Ringgold. TAR BEACH. 1988. *(page 204)*

300 Faith Ringgold. With detail of THE PURPLE
QUILT. 1986. *(page 205)*

Chapter Thirteen
Architecture and Environmental Design

Notes

301 Margaret Courtney-Clarke. BEAUTIFYING THE SPACE IN WHICH WE LIVE MAKES LIFE MORE BEARABLE. From *African Canvas,* Namibia, Africa. 1990. *(page 206)*

302 DOLMEN. Crocuno, north of Carnac, France. *(page 207)*

303 GREAT ZIMBABWE. Zimbabwe. Before 1450.
a. Plan. **b**. Interior. *(page 208)*

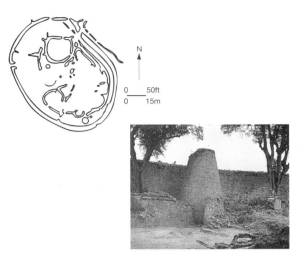

304 POST-AND-BEAM CONSTRUCTION. *(page 209)*

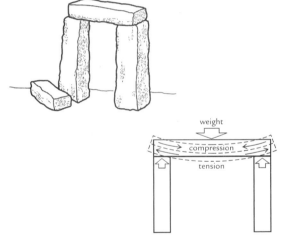

305 COLONNADE, COURT OF AMENHOTEP III. Temple of
Amun-Mut-Khonsu. View of the great court with double
row of papyrus-clustered columns. 18th dynasty. Luxor,
Thebes, Egypt. c. 1390 B.C.E. *(page 209)*

306 ROUND ARCH. *(page 210)*

keystone

307 BARREL VAULT. *(page 210)*

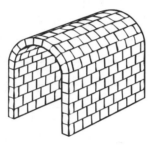

308 GROIN VAULT. *(page 210)*

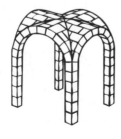

309 ARCADE. *(page 210)*

310 PONT DU GARD. Nimes, France. 15 C.E. *(page 210)*

311 DOME.   **a.** Dome (arch rotated 180°).   **b.** Dome on a cylinder.   **c.** Dome on pendentives. *(page 211)*

312 HAGIA SOPHIA. 532–535. **a.** Exterior.
b. Interior. *(page 211)*

313 NOTRE DAME DE CHARTRES. Chartres,
France. 1145–1513. *(page 212)*

314 GOTHIC ARCH. *(page 212)*

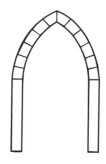

315 FLYING BUTTRESSES. *(page 212)*

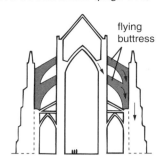

flying
buttress

316 TRUSSES. *(page 213)*

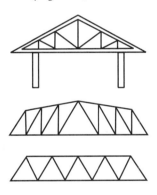

317 BALLOON FRAME. *(page 213)*

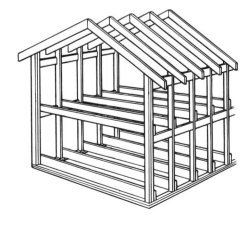

318 Joseph Paxton. CRYSTAL PALACE. London. 1850–1851. *(page 214)*

319 Louis Sullivan. WAINWRIGHT BUILDING. St. Louis, Missouri. 1890–1891. *(page 215)*

320 Le Corbusier. DOMINO CONSTRUCTION SYSTEM. 1914–1915. *(page 216)*

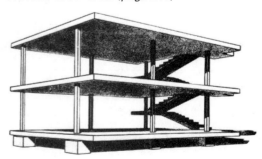

321 Walter Gropius. BAUHAUS. Dessau, Germany. 1925–1926. *(page 216)*

322 STEEL-FRAME CONSTRUCTION. *(page 217)*

323 Ludwig Mies van der Rohe and Philip Johnson. SEAGRAM BUILDING. New York. 1956–1958. *(page 217)*

324 Kenzo Tange. OLYMPIC STADIUMS (YOYOGI
SPORTS CENTER). **a.** Exterior, natatorium.
b. Interior, natataorium. **c.** Aerial view. *(page 218)*

325 SUSPENSION STRUCTURES. *(page 218)*

326 Eero Saarinen. SHELL STRUCTURE (TWA TERMINAL).
Kennedy Airport, N.Y. 1956–1962. *(page 219)*

327 FOLDED PLATE ROOF. *(page 219)*

328 PNEUMATIC STRUCTURE. *(page 219)*

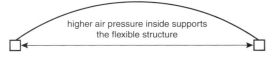

higher air pressure inside supports
the flexible structure

329 JEPPESEN TERMINAL BUILDING. Denver
International Airport. 1994. *(page 219)*

330 Zaha Hadid. *(page 220)*

331 Zaha Hadid. The Lois and Richard Rosenthal Center for Contemporary Art. CONTEMPORARY ARTS CENTER, Cincinnati, Ohio. 2003. *(page 220)*

332 Frank O. Gehry. GUGGENHEIM MUSEUM BILBAO. Bilbao, Spain. 1997. **a.** Interior. **b.** Exterior. *(page 221)*

333 Ken Smith. MOMA ROOF GARDEN, 2005.
(page 222)

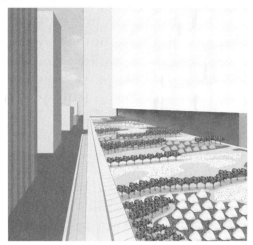

334 Frank Lloyd Wright. FALLING WATER
(EDGAR KAUFMANN RESIDENCE). Bear Run,
Pennsylvania. 1936. *(page 222)*

335 FRANK LLOYD WRIGHT. 1936. *(page 223)*

336 Mick Pearce. THE EASTGATE COMPLEX.
Harare, Zimbabwe, 1996.   **a.** Exterior.
b. Energy use. *(page 224)*

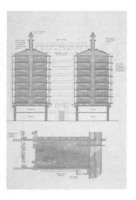

337 Glenn Murcutt. MAGNEY HOUSE, 1982–1984.
(page 225)

338 BREN SCHOOL OF ENVIRONMENTAL SCIENCE,
2002. *(page 225)*

339 Raymond Loewy. COLDSPOT SUPER SIX
REFRIGERATOR, 1934. *(page 226)*

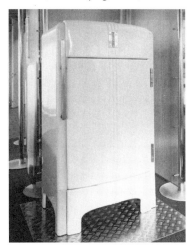

340 Sony Corporation. TR-610 TRANSISTOR-
RADIO, 1957. *(page 226)*

341 Frogdesign/Harmut Esslinger. APPLE
MACINTOSH, 1984. *(page 227)*

342 Lunar Design. ORAL-B CROSS-ACTION
TOOTHBRUSH, 1999. *(page 227)*

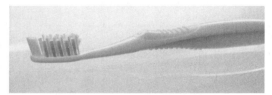

Part Four
Art as Cultural Heritage

Notes

Ma Yuan. WATCHING THE DEER BY A PINE
SHADED STREAM. c. 1200. *(page 229)*

Chapter Fourteen
From the Earliest Art to the Bronze Age

Notes

343 ENGRAVED OCHRE. From Blombos Cave, South Africa, c. 75,000 B.C.E. *(page 231)*

344 WOMAN OF WILLENDORF. c. 25,000–20,000 B.C.E. *(page 231)*

345 WOMAN OF LESPUGUE. **a.** back view
b. front view *(page 231)*

346 WALL PAINTING OF ANIMALS. Chauvet Cave,
Pont d'Arc, France. c. 28,000 B.C.E. *(page 232)*

347 DEER AND HANDS. Las Manos Cave,
Argentina. c. 15,000 B.C.E. *(page 233)*

348 EARTHENWARE BEAKER. Susa, Iran. c. 4000
B.C.E. *(page 234)*

349 AN EVOLUTION OF ABSTRACTION. From Neolithic
pottery, Shensi Province, China. *(page 235)*

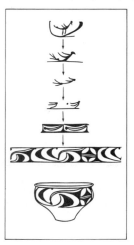

350 BURIAL URN. Kansu type. Chinese,
Neolithic period. c. 2200 B.C.E. *(page 235)*

351 PICTOGRAPHS TO WRITING, ASIAN AND
WESTERN. *(page 235)*

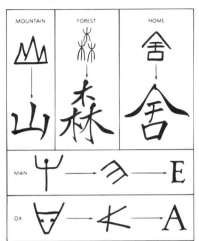

352 EARLIEST CENTERS OF CIVILIZATION, 3500–1500
B.C.E. *(page 236)*

353 ZIGGURAT OF UR-NAMMU. Iraq. c. 2100 B.C.E.
a. Reconstruction drawing. **b.** Incomplete
restoration. *(page 237)*

354 Reconstructed LYRE. From "The King's Grave" tomb RT 789, Ur. c. 2650–2550 B.C.E. **a.** Soundbox. **b.** Front plaque. *(page 237)*

355 HEAD OF AN AKKADIAN RULER. Nineveh. c. 2300–2200 B.C.E. *(page 238)*

356 THE GREAT PYRAMIDS. Giza, Egypt. Pyramid of Mycerinus, c. 2500 B.C.E.; Pyramid of Chefren, 2650 B.C.E.; Pyramid of Cheops, c. 2570 B.C.E. *(page 239)*

357 THE ANCIENT MIDDLE EAST. *(page 239)*

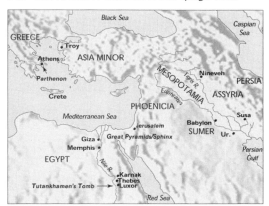

358 FUNERARY TEMPLE OF QUEEN HATSHEPSUT.
Deir el-Bahari. c. 1490–1460 B.C.E. *(page 239)*

359 KING MYCERINUS AND A QUEEN. KHAMERERNEBTY.
Egypt, Giza, Old Kingdom, Dynasty 4, reign of
Mycerinus, 2532–2510 B.C.E. *(page 240)*

360 MASK FROM MUMMY CASE. Tutankhamen.
c. 1340 B.C.E. *(page 240)*

361 WALL PAINTING FROM THE TOMB OF NEBAMUN.
Thebes, Egypt. c. 1450 B.C.E. *(page 241)*

Chapter Fifteen
The Classical and Medieval West

Notes

362 Exekias. GREEK VASE. Achilles and Ajax playing draughts. c. 540 B.C.E. *(page 242)*

363 KOUROS. Statue of a youth. c. 610–600 B.C.E. *(page 243)*

364 Polykleitos. SPEAR BEARER (DORYPHOROS).
Roman copy after Greek original bronze of
450–440 B.C.E. *(page 243)*

365 Ictinus and Callicrates. PARTHENON. Acropolis,
Athens. 448–432 B.C.E.   **a.** View from the northwest.
b. View from the southwest. *(page 244)*   **c.** PARTHENON
FRIEZE. Poseidon, Apollo, and Artemis. *(page 245)*

366 ARCHITECTURAL ORDERS. *(page 246)*

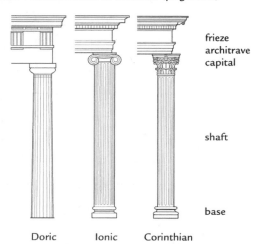

frieze
architrave
capital

shaft

base

Doric   Ionic   Corinthian

367 VENUS DE MEDICI. 3rd century B.C.E. *(page 246)*

_____

_____

_____

_____

_____

_____

_____

_____

_____

_____

_____

368 THE LAOCOÖN GROUP. Roman copy of a
1st- or 2nd-century B.C.E. *(page 247)*

_____

_____

_____

_____

_____

_____

_____

_____

_____

_____

_____

_____

369 FEMALE PORTRAIT. c. 54–117 C.E. *(page 248)*

_____

_____

_____

_____

_____

_____

_____

_____

_____

_____

_____

370 PANTHEON. Rome. 118–125 C.E. **a.** View of
the entrance. **b.** Plan. **c.** Section. *(page 249)*

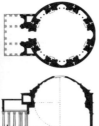

371 Giovanni Paolo Panini. THE INTERIOR OF
THE PANTHEON, ROME. c. 1734. *(page 249)*

372 EUROPE FROM 117 TO 1400. *(page 250)*

373 ROMAN PAINTING. Detail of west wall in a villa at Boscoreale. 1st century B.C.E. *(page 250)*

374 CHRIST TEACHING HIS DISCIPLES. Catacomb of Domitilla, Rome. Mid-4th century C.E. *(page 251)*

375 HEAD OF CONSTANTINE. c. 312 C.E. *(page 251)*

376 OLD ST. PETER'S BASILICA. Rome. c. 320–335.
a. Reconstruction drawing.   **b.** Interior view of
basilica of Old Saint Peter's.   **c.** Plan. *(page 252)*

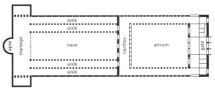

377 SAN VITALE. Ravenna, Italy. 526–547.
a. Exterior. **b.** Plan. **c.** EMPRESS THEODORA.
(page 253) **d.** Interior. *(page 254)*

378 CHRIST AS PANTOCRATOR WITH MARY AND
SAINTS. Apse mosaic. Cathedral of Monreale,
Sicily. Late 12th century. *(page 255)*

379 Andrei Rublev. OLD TESTAMENT TRINITY.
c. 1410–1420. *(page 256)*

380 Byzantine School. MADONNA AND CHILD ON A
CURVED THRONE. Byzantine, 13th century. *(page 256)*

381 SCYTHIAN ANIMAL. (BRIDLE PLAQUE WITH A BEAST
OF PREY CURVED ROUND). 5th century B.C.E. *(page 257)*

382 PURSE COVER. From the Sutton Hoo Ship Burial, Suffolk, England. Before 655. *(page 257)*

383 CHI-RHO MONOGRAM (XP). Page from the BOOK OF KELLS. Late 8th century. *(page 258)*

384 Detail of CHRIST OF THE PENTECOST. Saint Madeleine Cathedral, Vézelay, France. 1125–1150. *(page 259)*

385 NOTRE DAME DE CHARTRES. Chartres, France. 1145–1513. **a.** View from the southeast. *(page 260)* **b**. WEST FRONT.   **c**. "ROSE DE FRANCE" WINDOW. c. 1233. *(page 261)*   **d**. OLD TESTAMENT PROPHET, KINGS, AND QUEEN. c. 1145–1170. **e**. Plan based on Latin cross. *(page 262)*

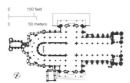

Chapter Sixteen
Renaissance and Baroque Europe

Notes

386 Giotto di Bondone. LAMENTATION. Scrovegni Chapel, Padua, Italy. c. 1305. *(page 264)*

387 Masaccio. THE HOLY TRINITY. Santa Maria Novella, Florence. 1425. *(page 265)*

388 Donatello. DAVID. c. 1425–1430. *(page 266)*

389 Donatello. MARY MAGDALEN. c. 1455. *(page 266)*

390 Sandro Botticelli. BIRTH OF VENUS. c. 1480. *(page 267)*

391 Leonardo da Vinci. THE INFANT IN THE
WOMB. c. 1510. *(page 268)*

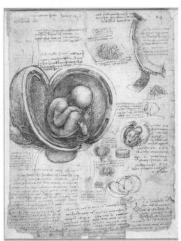

392 Leonardo da Vinci. MONA LISA. c. 1503–1506.
(page 268)

393 Leonardo da Vinci. THE LAST SUPPER. Santa Maria
delle Grazie, Milan. c. 1495–1498. **a.** Perspective lines
as both organizing structure and symbol of content.
b. Christ's figure as stable triangle, contrasting with
active turmoil of the disciples. *(page 269)*

394 Leonardo da Vinci. SELF-PORTRAIT. c. 1512.
(page 270)

395 Daniele da Volterra. MICHELANGELO
BUONARROTI. 1565. *(page 271)*

396 Michelangelo Buonarroti. **a.** DAVID. 1501–1504.
b. DAVID. Close-up of head. *(page 272)*

397 Michelangelo Buonarroti. Frescoes on the
ceiling and walls of THE SISTINE CHAPEL. Vatican,
Rome. 1508–1512. **a.** THE CREATION OF ADAM,
Fresco of the Sistine Chapel after restoration.
b. THE SISTINE CHAPEL after restoration. *(page 273)*

398 Raphael. MADONNA OF THE MEADOWS. 1505.
(page 274)

399 Jan van Eyck. THE MARRIAGE OF GIOVANNI
ARNOLFINI AND GIOVANNA CENAMI. 1434. *(page 275)*

400 Pieter Bruegel. THE RETURN OF THE HUNTERS. 1565. *(page 276)*

401 The Limbourg Brothers. FEBRUARY, from LES TRÈS RICHES HEURES DU DUC DE BERRY. 1413–1416. *(page 276)*

402 Andrea Palladio. VILLA ROTONDA. Vicenza, Italy. 1567–1570. *(page 277)*

403 Jacopo Tintoretto. THE LAST SUPPER.
1592–1594. *(page 278)*

404 Michelangelo Merisi da Caravaggio. THE
CONVERSION OF SAINT PAUL. 1600–1601. *(page 279)*

405 Gianlorenzo Bernini. DAVID. 1623. *(page 280)*

406 Gianlorenzo Bernini. THE ECSTASY OF SAINT TERESA. Detail of the altar, Cornaro Chapel, Santa Maria della Vittoria, Rome. 1645–1652. *(page 280)*

407 Peter Paul Rubens. THE RAISING OF THE CROSS. 1610–1611. *(page 281)*

408 Diego Velázquez. THE MAIDS OF HONOR. 1656. *(page 281)*

409 Rembrandt van Rijn. RETURN OF THE
PRODIGAL SON. c. 1668–1669. *(page 282)*

410 Rembrandt Harmensz van Rijn. SELF-PORTRAIT
LEANING ON A LEDGE. 1639. *(page 283)*

411 Jan Vermeer. THE GIRL WITH THE RED HAT.
c. 1665–1666. *(page 284)*

412 Jan Vermeer. THE KITCHEN MAID. c. 1658. *(page 284)*

413 VERSAILLES. c. 1665. Painting by Pierre Patel. *(page 285)*

414 Germain Boffrand. SALON DE LA PRINCESSE, HÔTEL DE SOUBISE. Paris. Begun 1732. *(page 285)*

415 Jean Honoré Fragonard. THE SWING. 1767. *(page 286)*

416 Sofonisba Anguissola. SELF-PORTRAIT. 1556. *(page 287)*

417 Artemisia Gentileschi. JUDITH AND THE MAIDSERVANT WITH THE HEAD OF HOLOFERNES. c. 1625. *(page 287)*

418 GHAZNI MINARET, Afghanistan. Early
twelfth century. *(page 288)*

_____

_____

_____

_____

_____

_____

_____

_____

_____

_____

_____

Chapter Seventeen
Traditional Arts of Asia

Notes

419 MALE TORSO. Harappā, Indus Valley.
c. 2400–2000 B.C.E. *(page 289)*

420 HISTORICAL MAP OF ASIA. *(page 290)*

421 a. GREAT STUPA. Sāñchī, India. 10 B.C.E.–15 C.E.
b. Eastern gate of THE GREAT STUPA. *(page 291)*

422 EVOLUTION OF BUDDHIST ARCHITECTURE.
a. Early Indian stupa. 3rd century to early 1st
century B.C.E. **b.** Later Indian stupa. 2nd century
C.E. **c.** Chinese pagoda. 5th to 7th centuries C.E.
d. Japanese pagoda. 7th century C.E. *(page 291)*

423 STANDING BODHISATTVA. N.W. Pakistan,
Gandhara region. Late 2nd century A.D. *(page 292)*

424 STANDING BUDDHA. 5th century. *(page 293)*

425 "BEAUTIFUL BODHISATTVA" PADMAPANI.
Detail of a fresco from Cave 1. Ajanta, India.
c. 600–650. *(page 293)*

426 KANDARYA MAHADEVA TEMPLE. Khajuráho,
India. 10th–11th centuries. **a.** Exterior
b. Scene from KANDARIYA MAHADEVA TEMPLE.
Chandella dynasty, 1025–50 C.E. *(page 294)*

427 NĀTARĀJA: SHIVA AS KING SHIVA
NĀTARĀJA, LORD OF THE DANCE. South India,
Chola Period, 11th century. *(page 295)*

428 THE APPROACH OF KRISHNA, c. 1660–1670.
(page 296)

429 BOROBUDUR. Java. c. 800. **a.** Aerial view.
b. CORRIDOR AT BOROBUDUR. First Gallery. *(page 297)*

430 ANGKOR WAT. c. 1120–1150. **a.** West entrance. **b.** Plan. *(page 298)*

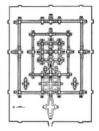

431 RITUAL VESSEL (LA TIGRESSE). China. Shang dynasty. c. 1100–1000 B.C.E. *(page 299)*

432 TERRA COTTA WARRIORS. Pit No. 1, Museum of the First Emperor of Qin. Shaanxi Province, China. Qin Dynasty. c. 210 B.C.E. *(page 300)*

433 FLYING HORSE. Eastern Han dynasty. 2nd century. *(page 301)*

434 MIRROR WITH XIWANGMU, Early Six Dynasties Period (317–581). *(page 302)*

435 Huai-su. Detail of AUTOBIOGRAPHY. Tang dynasty, 7th–10th centuries. *(page 303)*

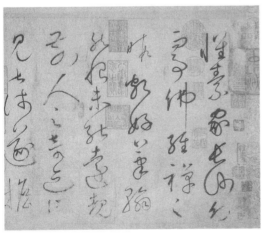

436 Fan Kuan. TRAVELERS AMONG MOUNTAINS
AND STREAMS. Song dynasty. Early 11th
century. *(page 304)*

437 Ma Yuan. WATCHING THE DEER BY A PINE
SHADED STREAM, c. 1200. *(page 305)*

438 Wu Chen. ALBUM LEAF FROM MANUAL OF
INK BAMBOO. 1350. *(page 305)*

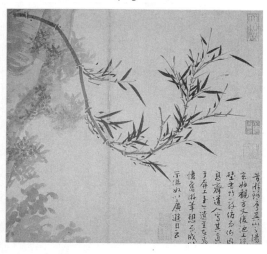

439 Tang Yin. WHISPERING PINES ON A MOUNTAIN
PATH. Ming dynasty. c. 1516. *(page 306)*

440 PORCELAIN PLATE. Mid-14th century. *(page 307)*

441 WINE PITCHER. Korea. Koryo dynasty. Mid-
12th century. *(page 307)*

442 AVATAMASKA SUTRA, Vol. 12, 13th–14th century. *(page 308)*

443 Bada Shanren. CICADA ON A BANANA LEAF. Qing dynasty. 1688–1689. *(page 309)*

444 MAIN SHRINE. Ise, Japan. c. 685. *(page 309)*

445 HORYUJI TEMPLE. Nara, Japan. c. 690.
a. Pagoda and a section of the lecture hall (Kondo).
b. KONDO, Structural diagram. *(page 310)*

446 Unkei. Detail of MUCHAKU. c. 1208. *(page 311)*

447 BURNING OF THE SANJO PALACE. From the
HEIJI MONOGATARI EMAKI (illustrated Scrolls of
the Events of the Heiji Era), Japan. Second half
of the 13th century. *(page 311)*

448 Sesshū. HABOKU LANDSCAPE. *(page 312)*

449 Tawaraya Sōtatsu. WAVES AT MATSUSHIMA.
17th century. *(page 313)*

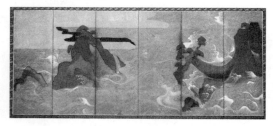

450 Utamaro Kitagawa. REFLECTED BEAUTY, SEVEN
BEAUTIES APPLYING MAKE-UP: OKITA c. 1790. *(page 314)*

451 KATSURA DETACHED PALACE. Kyoto, Japan.
17th century. **a.** Gardens and tea house.
b. Imperial villa and gardens. **c.** Interior of
tea house. *(page 315)*

452 Mitsutani Kunishiro. UPSTAIRS. 1910.
(page 316)

Chapter Eighteen
The Islamic World

Notes

453 GREAT MOSQUE. Kairouan, Tunisia.
836–875. *(page 318)*

454 PITCHER (SPOUTED EWER). Kashan. Early
13th century. *(page 318)*

455 TEXT OF THE KORAN. North Africa or
Spain. 11th century. *(page 319)*

456 COURT OF THE LIONS, ALHAMBRA. Granada,
Spain. 1309–1354. *(page 319)*

457 THE ISLAMIC WORLD. *(page 320)*

458 MIHRAB. Persia (Iran). c. 1354. *(page 320)*

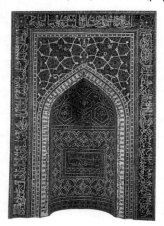

459 MIR-I-ARAB MADRASA. Bukhara, Uzbekistan. 1535–1536. *(page 321)*

460 Attributed to Sultan-Muhammad. SULTAN SANJAR AND THE OLD WOMAN, from the KHAMSEH (FIVE POEMS) of Nizami, folio 181, 1539–1543. *(page 322)*

461 Mansur. TURKEY-COCK. c. 1612. *(page 323)*

462 TAJ MAHAL. Agra, India. 1632–1648. *(page 323)*

463 HEAD FROM WARKA. Displayed by Iraqi authorities after its recovery. 3500–3000 B.C.E. *(page 324)*

Chapter Nineteen
Africa, Oceania, and the Americas

Notes

464 AFRICA. *(page 325)*

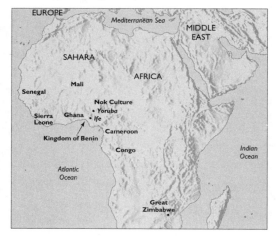

465 HEAD. Nok culture, Nigeria. 500 B.C.E.–200 C.E. *(page 326)*

466 MALE PORTRAIT HEAD. Ife, Nigeria. 13th century. *(page 326)*

467 BENIN HEAD. Nigeria. 16th century. *(page 326)*

468 PENDANT MASK. Nigeria. Early 16th century. *(page 327)*

469 TYI WARA DANCERS. Mali. *(page 327)*

470 LARGE DANCE HEADDRESS. Bamenda area, Cameroon, Africa. 19th century. *(page 328)*

471 Olembe Alaye. HOUSE POST. Yoruba, Nigeria. Mid-20th century. *(page 328)*

472 TOMB OF FORMER CHIEF LISA. Ondo, Nigeria.
The *House Post* is third from left. *(page 329)*

473 POWER FIGURE (NKONDE). Kongo people.
Democratic Republic of Congo, 19th–20th
century. *(page 329)*

474 ADINKRA CLOTH (detail). Asante, Ghana.
(page 330)

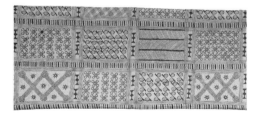

475 TEXTILE (KPOKPO). Mende peoples, Sierra Leone and Liberia. *(page 330)*

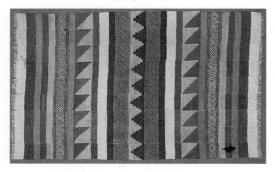

476 Detail of ADIRE CLOTH. Yoruba, Lagos, Nigeria. 1984. *(page 330)*

477 PROTECTIVE PROW FIGURE FROM A WAR CANOE. New Georgia Island, Solomon Islands. 19th century. *(page 331)*

478 OCEANIA AND AUSTRALIA. *(page 332)*

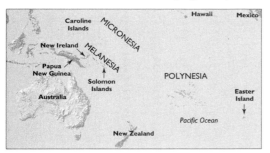

479 MASK. New Ireland. c. 1920. *(page 332)*

480 COCONUT GRATER. Kapingamarangi,
Caroline Islands. 1954. *(page 332)*

481 STANDING FEMALE FIGURE. Nukuoro Atoll, Central Carolines. 19th century. *(page 333)*

482 MOAI. Easter Island. *(page 333)*

483 AUMAKUA. Wooden image from Forbes Cave, Hawaii. *(page 333)*

484 MAORI MEETING HOUSE. Called "Ruatepupuke." New Zealand. 1881. **a**. Front view. **b**. Ridge pole. *(page 334)*

485 Bunia. FUNERARY RITES AND SPIRIT'S PATHWAY AFTER DEATH. Australian bark painting. Groote Eylantdt, Arnhem Land. Northern Australia. *(page 335)*

486 AMERICAS. *(page 336)*

487 GREAT SERPENT MOUND. Ohio. Adena
culture. 100 B.C.E.–500 C.E. *(page 336)*

488 HAND-SHAPED CUTOUT. Hopewell Mound,
Ohio. c. 150. *(page 337)*

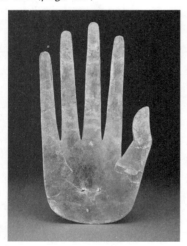

489 BLANKET, BANDED BACKGROUND. Navajo.
1870–1875. *(page 337)*

490 JAR. Ácoma Pueblo. c. 1850–1900. *(page 338)*

491 Marshall Lomakema. HOPI KACHINA, HUMIS KATSINA FIGURE. 1971. *(page 339)*

492 POMO FEATHER BASKET. California. 1937. *(page 339)*

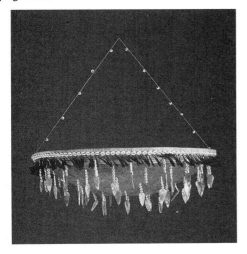

493 Mato Tope (Four Bears). ROBE WITH MATO TOPE'S EXPLOITS. c. 1835. *(page 340)*

494 TLINGIT COMMUNITY HOUSE. Ketchikan, Alaska. *(page 340)*

495 Howling Wolf. CLASSROOM AT FORT MARION. 1876. (page 341)

496 PYRAMID OF THE SUN. Teotihuacan.
1st–7th century C.E. *(page 342)*

497 Detail of TEMPLE OF THE FEATHERED
SERPENT. Teotihuacan. 150–200 C.E. *(page 342)*

498 TEMPLE I. Maya. Tikal, Guatemala. c. 300–900 C.E.
(page 343)

499 LINTEL 24. Yaxchilan, Maya. 709 C.E.
(page 343)

500 CHACMOOL. 10th–12th century. *(page 344)*

501 VESSEL OF THE FEATHERED SERPENT
QUETZALCOATL. Aztec. 1450–1521. *(page 344)*

502 MACHU PICCHU. Inca. Peru. Early 16th century.
(page 344)

503 HUMMINGBIRD. Nazca Valley, Peru.
(page 345)

504 KERO CUP. Peru. Late 16th–17th century.
(page 345)

505 FEATHERED SERPENT AND FLOWERING
TREES. Probably Metepec, A.D.–750,
Teotihuacan, Techinantitla, Mexico. *(page 346)*

Part Five
The Modern World

Notes

Fujishima Takeji. SUNRISE OVER THE EASTERN SEA. 1932. *(page 347)*

Chapter Twenty
Late Eighteenth
and Nineteenth Centuries

Notes

506 Jacques-Louis David. OATH OF THE HORATII. 1784. *(page 349)*

507 Angelica Kauffmann. CORNELIA, POINTING TO HER CHILDREN AS HER TREASURES. c. 1785. *(page 349)*

508 Thomas Jefferson. MONTICELLO.
Charlottesville, Virginia. 1793–1806. *(page 350)*

509 Francisco de Goya y Lucientes. THE THIRD
OF MAY 1808. 1814. *(page 351)*

510 J. M. W. Turner. THE BURNING OF THE HOUSES
OF LORDS AND COMMONS, 1834. *(page 352)*

511 Thomas Cole. THE OXBOW. 1836. *(page 353)*

512 Robert S. Duncanson. BLUE HOLE, LITTLE MIAMI RIVER. 1851. *(page 353)*

513 Eugène Delacroix. THE DEATH OF SARDANAPALUS. 1827. *(page 354)*

514 Carleton E. Watkins. THE THREE BROTHERS—
4480 FEET—YOSEMITE. 1861. *(page 355)*

515 Nadar (Félix Tournachon). SARAH BERNHARDT.
1855. *(page 356)*

516 Gustave Courbet. THE STONE BREAKERS.
1849 (destroyed in 1945). *(page 357)*

517 Rosa Bonheur. THE HORSE FAIR.
1853–1855. *(page 358)*

518 Rosa Bonheur. STUDY FOR THE HORSE
FAIR. c. 1853. *(page 358)*

519 W. H. Mote. ROSA BONHEUR. 1856. *(page 359)*

520 Jean Léon Gérôme. PYGMALION AND
GALATEA. c. 1860. *(page 360)*

521 Thomas Eakins. WILLIAM RUSH CARVING
HIS ALLEGORICAL FIGURE OF THE SCHUYLKILL
RIVER. 1876–1877. *(page 360)*

522 Henry Ossawa Tanner. THE BANJO LESSON.
1893. *(page 361)*

523 Edouard Manet. LUNCHEON ON THE GRASS
(LE DÉJEUNER SUR L'HERBE). 1863. *(page 362)*

524 Claude Monet. ON THE BANK OF THE
SEINE, BENNECOURT. 1868. *(page 363)*

525 Claude Monet. IMPRESSION: SUNRISE.
1872. *(page 364)*

526 CLAUDE MONET on his eightieth birthday.
1920. *(page 365)*

527 Pierre-Auguste Renoir. THE LUNCHEON OF
THE BOATING PARTY. 1876. *(page 366)*

528 Edgar Degas. THE BALLET CLASS. c. 1879–1880.
(page 367)

529 Mary Cassatt. THE BOATING PARTY. 1893–1894. *(page 368)*

530 Auguste Rodin. THE THINKER (LE PENSEUR). c. 1910. *(page 369)*

531 Georges Seurat. A SUNDAY ON LA GRANDE JATTE. 1884–1886. *(page 370)*

532 Paul Cézanne. MONT SAINTE-VICTOIRE.
1902–1904. *(page 371)*

533 Paul Cézanne. SELF-PORTRAIT. *(page 372)*

534 Vincent van Gogh, after Hiroshige. JAPONAISERIE:
FLOWERING PLUM TREE. 1887. *(page 373)*

535 Vincent van Gogh. THE SOWER. 1888. *(page 373)*

536 Vincent van Gogh. THE STARRY NIGHT. 1889. *(page 374)*

537 Paul Gauguin. THE VISION AFTER THE SERMON (JACOB WRESTLING WITH THE ANGEL). 1888. *(page 375)*

538 Paul Gauguin. FATATA TE MITI (BY THE SEA). 1892. *(page 376)*

539 Paul Gauguin. PORTRAIT OF THE ARTIST WITH THE IDOL. c. 1893. *(page 377)*

540 Henri de Toulouse-Lautrec. AT THE MOULIN ROUGE. 1892–1895. *(page 378)*

541 Edvard Munch. THE SCREAM. 1893.
(page 379)

_____

_____

_____

_____

_____

_____

_____

_____

_____

_____

_____

Chapter Twenty-One
Early Twentieth Century

542 Henri Matisse. LA DESSERTE. 1897. *(page 381)*

543 Henri Matisse. HARMONY IN RED. 1908–1909. *(page 381)*

544 Henri Matisse. JOY OF LIFE. 1905–1906. *(page 382)*

545 André Derain. LONDON BRIDGE. 1906. *(page 383)*

546 Ernst Ludwig Kirchner. STREET, BERLIN. 1913. *(page 384)*

547 Wassily Kandinsky. BLUE MOUNTAIN (DER BLAUE BERG). 1908–1909. *(page 385)*

548 Wassily Kandinsky. WITH THE BLACK ARCH NO. 154. 1912. *(page 385)*

549 Pablo Picasso. LES DEMOISELLES D'AVIGNON. 1907. *(page 386)*

550 KOTA RELIQUARY FIGURE. Cameroon, probably 20th century. *(page 387)*

551 MASK FROM IVORY COAST. *(page 387)*

552 Paul Cézanne. GARDANNE. 1885–1886. *(page 387)*

553 Georges Braque. HOUSES AT L'ESTAQUE.
1908. *(page 387)*

554 Georges Braque. THE PORTUGUESE. 1911.
(page 388)

555 Pablo Picasso. GUITAR. Paris, winter 1912–1913.
(page 389)

556 Pablo Picasso. VIOLIN AND FRUIT. 1913.
(page 389)

557 PICASSO IN HIS STUDIO AT CANNES. c. 1965.
(page 390)

558 Constantin Brancusi. SLEEP. 1908. *(page 391)*

559 Constantin Brancusi. SLEEPING MUSE I.
1909–1911. *(page 391)*

560 Constantin Brancusi. THE NEWBORN. 1915.
(page 391)

561 CYCLADIC II. Female statuette. 2700–2300 B.C.E.
(page 391)

562 Constantin Brancusi. BIRD IN SPACE. 1928.
(page 392)

563 Alfred Stieglitz. THE STEERAGE. 1907.
(page 393)

564 Georgia O'Keeffe. LIGHT COMING ON THE
PLAINS NO II. 1917. *(page 393)*

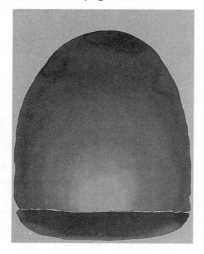

565 Frank Lloyd Wright. ROBIE HOUSE.
Chicago, Illinois. 1909. *(page 394)*

566 Giacomo Balla. ABSTRACT SPEED—THE
CAR HAS PASSED. 1913. *(page 395)*

567 Umberto Boccioni. UNIQUE FORMS OF
CONTINUITY IN SPACE. 1913. *(page 395)*

568 Marcel Duchamp. NUDE DESCENDING A
STAIRCASE, NO. 2, 1912. *(page 396)*

569 Sonia Delaunay. BAL BULLIER. 1913. *(page 396)*

Chapter Twenty-Two
Between World Wars

Notes

570 Marcel Duchamp. L.H.O.O.Q 1919. *(page 398)*

571 Man Ray. (THE GIFT). c. 1958. *(page 399)*

572 Raoul Hausmann. THE SPIRIT OF OUR TIME. 1919. *(page 399)*

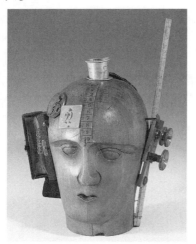

573 Hannah Höch. THE MULTI-MILLIONAIRE. 1923. *(page 399)*

574 Paul Klee. INSULA DULCAMARA. 1938. *(page 400)*

575 Henry Moore. RECUMBENT FIGURE. 1938.
(page 401)

576 Giorgio De Chirico. THE MYSTERY AND
MELANCHOLY OF A STREET. 1914. *(page 401)*

577 Salvador Dali. THE PERSISTENCE OF MEMORY.
1931. *(page 402)*

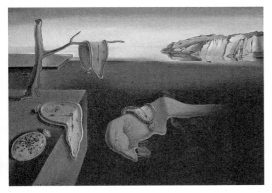

578 Joan Miró. WOMAN HAUNTED BY THE PASSAGE OF THE DRAGONFLY, BIRD OF BAD OMEN. 1938. *(page 403)*

579 René Magritte. PORTRAIT. 1935. *(page 403)*

580 Frida Kahlo. THE TWO FRIDAS. 1939. *(page 403)*

581 Frida Kahlo. SELF-PORTRAIT WITH CROPPED
HAIR. 1940. *(page 404)*

582 Fernand Léger. THE CITY. 1919. *(page 405)*

583 Kasimir Malevich. SUPREMATIST COMPOSITION:
AIRPLANE FLYING. 1915. *(page 406)*

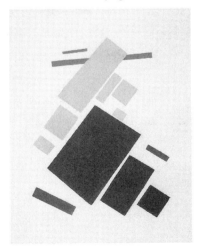

584 Tarsila do Amaral. ABAPORU. 1928. *(page 406)*

585 Vladimir Tatlin. MODEL FOR MONUMENT TO THE THIRD INTERNATIONAL. 1919–1920. *(page 407)*

586 Piet Mondrian. COMPOSITION WITH RED, BLUE, AND YELLOW. 1930. *(page 408)*

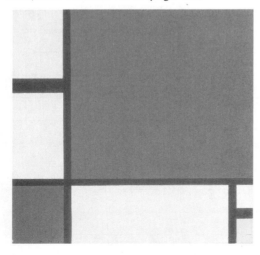

587 Piet Mondrian. BROADWAY BOOGIE-WOOGIE. 1942–1943. *(page 408)*

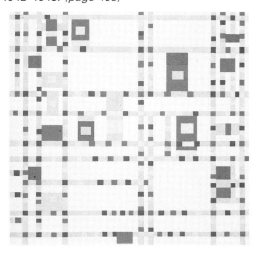

588 Gerrit Rietveld. SCHRÖDER HOUSE, UTRECHT. 1924. *(page 409)*

589 Le Corbusier. VILLA SAVOYE. Poissy, France. 1928–1930. *(page 409)*

590 Max Beckmann. DEPARTURE. 1932–1933.
(page 410)

591 Pablo Picasso. GUERNICA. 1937. *(page 411)*

592 Vera Mukhina. MONUMENT TO THE
PROLETARIAT AND AGRICULTURE. 1937. *(page 412)*

593 Diego Rivera. THE LIBERATION OF THE PEON. 1931. *(page 413)*

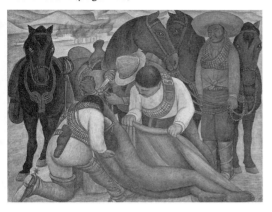

594 DIEGO RIVERA AND FRIDA KAHLO. c. 1930. *(page 414)*

595 Dorothea Lange. WHITE ANGEL BREAD LINE, SAN FRANCISCO. 1933. *(page 415)*

596 Edward Hopper. NIGHTHAWKS. 1942.
(page 415)

597 Grant Wood. AMERICAN GOTHIC. 1930. *(page 416)*

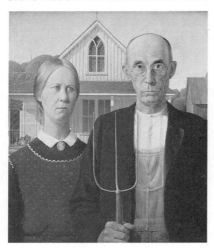

598 Thomas Hart Benton. PALISADES, FROM THE
SERIES AMERICAN HISTORICAL EPIC. C. 1919–1924.
(page 417)

599 Sargent Johnson. FOREVER FREE. 1933.
(page 417)

600 Jacob Lawrence. GENERAL TOUSSAINT
L'OUVERTURE DEFEATS THE ENGLISH AT SALINE.
1937–1938. *(page 418)*

601 Archibald Motley, Jr. BARBECUE. 1934. *(page 418)*

Chapter Twenty-Three
Postwar Modern Movements in the West

602 Hans Namuth. JACKSON POLLOCK. 1950.
(page 420)

603 Jackson Pollock. AUTUMN RHYTHM.
(NUMBER 30), 1950. *(page 420)*

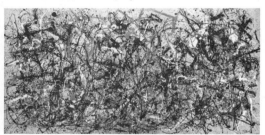

604 Mark Rothko. BLUE, ORANGE, RED. 1961. *(page 421)*

605 Helen Frankenthaler. MOUNTAINS AND SEA. 1952. *(page 421)*

606 Robert Motherwell. ELEGY TO THE SPANISH REPUBLIC NO. 34, 1953–1954. *(page 422)*

607 Willem de Kooning. WOMAN AND BICYCLE.
1952–1953. *(page 423)*

608 Norman Lewis. UNTITLED. c. 1947. *(page 423)*

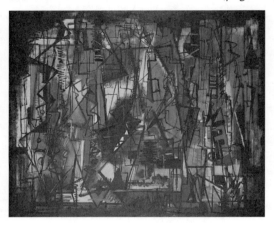

609 Asger Jorn. THE GREAT VICTORY. 1955–1956.
(page 424)

610 Alberto Burri. COMPOSITION, 1953. *(page 424)*

611 David Smith. CUBI XVII. 1963. *(page 425)*

612 Harry Callahan. MULTIPLE TREES. 1949.
(page 425)

613 Skidmore, Owings, and Merrill. LEVER
HOUSE. 1952. *(page 426)*

614 Oscar Niemeyer. PLANALTO PALACE. Presidential
Residence, Brasília, Brazil. 1960. *(page 426)*

615 Robert Rauschenberg. MONOGRAM.
1955–1959. *(page 427)*

616 Robert Rauschenberg. CANYON. 1959.
(page 427)

617 ROBERT RAUSCHENBERG. *(page 428)*

618 Robert Rauschenberg. TRACER. 1963.
(page 429)

619 Jasper Johns. TARGET WITH FOUR FACES. 1955. *(page 429)*

620 Niki de Saint Phalle. ST. SEBASTIAN, OR THE PORTRAIT OF MY LOVE. 1960. *(page 430)*

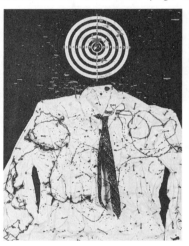

621 Jean Tinguely. HOMAGE TO NEW YORK: A SELF-CONSTRUCTING, SELF-DESTRUCTING WORK OF ART. 1960. *(page 431)*

622 Allan Kaprow. HOUSEHOLD. Happening
commissioned by Cornell University,
performed May 1964. *(page 432)*

623 Richard Hamilton. JUST WHAT IS IT THAT
MAKES TODAY'S HOMES SO DIFFERENT, SO
APPEALING? 1959. *(page 433)*

624 James Rosenquist. F-III. 1965. *(page 432)*
(page 433)

625 Andy Warhol. MARILYN DIPTYCH. 1962.
(page 434)

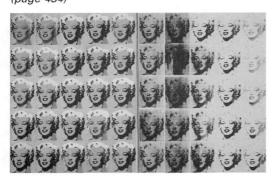

626 Roy Lichtenstein. DROWNING GIRL. 1963.
(page 435)

627 Claes Oldenburg. TWO CHEESEBURGERS WITH
EVERYTHING (DUAL HAMBURGERS). 1962. *(page 435)*

628 Donald Judd. UNTITLED. 1967. *(page 436)*

629 Ellsworth Kelly. BLUE, GREEN, YELLOW, ORANGE, RED. 1966. *(page 437)*

630 Frank Stella. AGBATANA III. 1968. *(page 437)*

631 Joseph Kosuth. ONE AND THREE CHAIRS. 1965. *(page 438)*

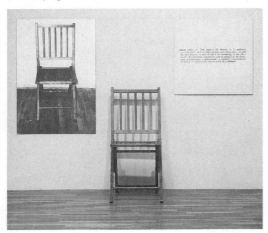

632 Christo and Jeanne-Claude. RUNNING FENCE. SONOMA AND MARIN COUNTIES, California. 1972–1976. *(page 439)*

633 Walter De Maria. THE LIGHTNING FIELD. Quemado, New Mexico. 1977. *(page 439)*

634 Robert Smithson. SPIRAL JETTY. Great Salt Lake, Utah. 1970. *(page 440)*

635 James Turrell. AMBA. 1982. *(page 441)*

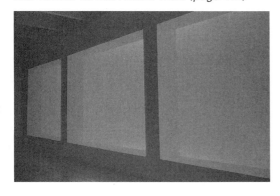

636 Andy Goldsworthy. STORM KING WALL. 1997–1998. *(page 441)*

637 Judy Chicago. THE DINNER PARTY. 1979.
(page 443)

638 Nancy Spero. REBIRTH OF VENUS. Detail.
1984. *(page 443)*

639 Louise Bourgeois. THE DESTRUCTION OF
THE FATHER. 1974. *(page 444)*

640 Joseph Beuys. COYOTE: I LIKE AMERICA AND AMERICA LIKES ME. 1974. *(page 445)*

641 Ana Mendieta. TREE OF LIFE SERIES. 1977. *(page 445)*

642 Mierle Laderman Ukeles. A.I.R. WASH. 1974. *(page 445)*

643 Chris Ofili. THE HOLY VIRGIN MARY. 1996.
(page 446)

_____

_____

_____

_____

_____

_____

_____

_____

_____

_____

_____

Chapter Twenty-Four
Modern Art Beyond the West

Notes

644 Fujishima Takeji. SUNRISE OVER THE
EASTERN SEA. 1932. *(page 448)*

645 Saburo Murakami. PASSING THROUGH (21
PANELS OF 42 PAPERS). 1956. *(page 448)*

646 Gao Jianfu. THE FIVE-STORIED TOWER. 1926.
(page 449)

647 Li Hua. TAKE HIM IN! 1946. *(page 450)*

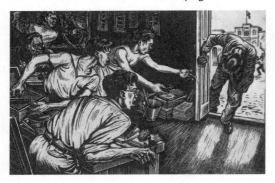

648 Amrita Sher-Gil. THE SWING. 1940. *(page 451)*

649 M. F. Husain. MAN. 1951. *(page 451)*

650 Mahmoud Mukhtar. EGYPT AWAKENING. 1919–1928. *(page 452)*

651 Ibrahim el-Salahi. FUNERAL AND A CRESCENT. 1963. *(page 453)*

652 Gerard Sekoto. STREET SCENE. 1945.
(page 453)

653 Uche Okeke. THE GROVE OF LIFE. 1962.
(page 454)

Part Six
The Postmodern World

Notes

Greg Lynn and Fabian Marcaccio, THE
PREDATOR. 2001. *(page 455)*

Chapter Twenty-Five
Postmodernity and Global Art

Notes

654 Johnson and Burgee. A.T. & T. BUILDING. New York City. 1978–1984. *(page 457)*

655 Michael Graves. PUBLIC SERVICES BUILDING. Portland, Oregon. 1980–1982. *(page 458)*

656 Rem Koolhaas. SEATTLE CENTRAL LIBRARY.
2004. *(page 458)*

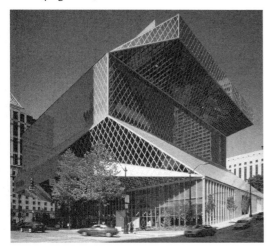

657 Susan Rothenberg. BLUE HEAD. 1980–1981.
(page 459)

658 Eric Fischl. UNTITLED. 1986. *(page 459)*

659 Anselm Kiefer. OSIRIS AND ISIS. 1985–1987. *(page 460)*

660 Elizabeth Murray. MORE THAN YOU KNOW. 1983. *(page 461)*

661 Kerry James Marshall. BETTER HOMES BETTER GARDENS. 1994. *(page 461)*

662 Andreas Gursky. STATEVILLE, ILLINOIS.
2002. *(page 462)*

663 Carrie Mae Weems. ANCIENT RUINS OF TIME,
from series DREAMING IN CUBA. 2002. *(page 463)*

664 Cindy Sherman. UNTITLED FILM STILL #48.
1979. *(page 463)*

665 Martin Puryear. OLD MOLE. 1985. *(page 464)*

666 Anish Kapoor. TO REFLECT AN INTIMATE PART OF THE RED. 1981. *(page 464)*

667 Kiki Smith. ICE MAN. 1995. *(page 465)*

668 Matthew Barney. THE CABINET OF HARRY
HOUDINI, from CREMASTER 2. 1999. *(page 465)*

669 Maya Lin. VIETNAM VETERANS MEMORIAL.
The Mall, Washington, D.C. 1980–1982. *(page 466)*

670 R. M. Fischer. RECTOR GATE. 1988. *(page 467)*

671 Mierle Laderman Ukeles. THE SOCIAL
MIRROR. New York. 1983. *(page 468)*

672 Richard Misrach. SUBMERGED LAMPPOST,
SALTON SEA. 1985. *(page 468)*

673 Barbara Kruger. UNTITLED (I SHOP
THEREFORE I AM). 1987. *(page 469)*

674 Fred Wilson. MINING THE MUSEUM. 1992. *(page 469)*

675 William Kentridge. Drawing from HISTORY OF THE MAIN COMPLAINT. (Title Page). 1996. *(page 470)*

676 Mariko Mori. WAVE UFO. 2003. *(page 471)*

677 Jaune Quick-to-See Smith. THE RED MEAN:
SELF-PORTRAIT. 1992. *(page 471)*

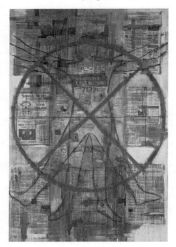

678 Shahzia Sikander. PLEASURE PILLARS. 2001.
(page 472)

679 Shirin Neshat. PASSAGE. 2001. *(page 472)*

680 Fodé Camara. PARCOURS–TRICOLORE II. 1988. *(page 473)*

681 Greg Lynn and Fabian Marcaccio. THE PREDATOR. 2001. *(page 473)*

682 Rafael Lozano-Hemmer. VECTORIAL ELEVATION. 1999–2000. *(page 474)*

683 Santiago Calatrava. WORLD TRADE CENTER
TRANSPORTATION HUB. 2006–2009. *(page 475)*